D0578521

PATCHWORK FOR BEGINNERS

First published by V&A Publishing, 2009
V&A Publishing
Victoria and Albert Museum
South Kensington
London SW7 2RL

Hardback edition
ISBN 978 1 85177 596 5
Library of Congress Control Number 2009932294

10 9 8 7 6 5 4 3 2 1
2014 2013 2012 2011 2010

A catalogue record for this book is available
from the British Library.

Illustrations: Polly Scott Bolton at Polly Hope Textiles
Designer: Turnbull Grey
Copy-editor: Miranda Harrison
New photography by Peter Kelleher, Richard Davis and Pip Barnard
V&A Photography by V&A Photographic Studio

Jacket illustration: From a selection of fabrics and
textiles from the V&A; artwork by Turnbull Grey
Frontispiece: Anyone can set up a patchwork group! All the
members of the V&A Patchwork Club work at the Museum and
share their enthusiasm for making patchwork.

Printed in Hong Kong

V&A Publishing
Victoria and Albert Museum
South Kensington
London SW7 2RL
www.vam.ac.uk

PATCHWORK FOR BEGINNERS

SUE PRICHARD

V&A Publishing

CONTENTS

FOREWORD

The aim of this book is to provide an introduction and guide to making patchwork for the absolute beginner. It combines ideas for small projects with stunning images of selected objects in the V&A's collection to inspire you to think about colour, pattern and design. Basic patchwork patterns are provided with simple, easy-to-follow instructions on different styles and techniques. The technical information can be used as a platform to progress to larger, more ambitious projects, including bed covers. We hope you will enjoy mastering the step-by-step guides, and go on to create your own beautiful heirlooms of the future.

Embroidered pin cushion and purse, English, 1600–29. V&A: 316-1898

Embroidered
needlecase and cover,
British, 1700–50.
V&A: T.11-1943

GLOSSARY

This simple glossary explains all the terms used in this book. It will also help you to navigate your way through any specialist shop, magazine or patchwork class with confidence.

APPLIQUÉ
A technique of layering one or more fabrics on top of a larger piece of fabric, creating a design.

FAT QUARTERS
Pre-cut bundles of fabric, sold by specialist suppliers.

MOSAIC PATCHWORK (ALSO KNOWN AS ENGLISH PAPER PIECING)
Patchwork that has been made by sewing fabric on to paper templates.

OVERSTITCH (ALSO KNOWN AS WHIPSTITCH)
A series of regular, close together stitches worked by hand, picking up the smallest possible amount of material underneath. Useful for a firm and secure edge.

PIECING
The process of sewing together the patchwork pieces.

ROSETTE
A central patchwork hexagon, surrounded by a circle of six further hexagons.

TACK/BASTE
To fasten or attach with a loose, temporary stitch (known as tacking or basting); primarily used to hold fabric to paper templates.

TEMPLATE
The cardboard or metal shape used as a pattern for cutting out the papers and fabric.

SEAM ALLOWANCE
The space between the edge of the fabric and the stitching line.

SELVEDGE
The edge of the fabric that is woven so that it will not unravel or fray. Here you will find the name of the design and the name of the manufacturer.

STRAIGHT OF GRAIN/GRAIN LINE
The woven threads in a fabric that run parallel to, or at right angles to, the selvedge.

WADDING
Material for padding also known as stuffing, batting or fibrefill.

Reverse of printed
cotton coverlet,
English, 1829.
V&A: T.428-1985

INTRODUCTION

Dear Sylvia.
Could any of your readers tell me the way to work silk
patchwork for sofa cushions etc. I have no idea whatever of
the cutting out, arranging, or putting together: also how to
make it into what is called mosaic work by working stars and
other things on it with crewel silks. Full particulars would
greatly oblige.
Mabel

(Sylvia's Home Journal, 1884)

Patchwork is one of the most creative of all crafts. The author of the above letter would have been reassured to know that it is also one of the easiest crafts to learn. There are numerous beautifully illustrated books to guide you through some of the more ambitious and technically accomplished examples. However, Practical Patchwork for Beginners will introduce you to the basic skills needed to produce charming and individual pieces, which you can treasure forever.

The origins of patchwork are lost in the mists of time. Fragments from many centuries have been discovered during archaeological excavations. In Britain, the most exquisite examples of patchwork date from the eighteenth century. The intricate and carefully stitched bed curtains and coverlets testify to the extraordinary skill of the makers – and also to the abundance of exuberant and brightly coloured fabrics that were available. The most decorative and precious examples have been lovingly cherished and handed down through the generations. The fabrics and design of each piece is as unique as its maker and the personal narrative which often documents its past. Memories and myth-making are bound up with the making of patchwork, from the stitching of love letters and wills into patchwork quilts to the assertion that kings slept soundly under a family heirloom. The making of patchwork is more than the piecing together of scraps of fabric. It is the means of passing down your own personal heritage to the next generation.

Dear Faith
I wanted dear G. Parents things kept in the family ... G.
Mother's quilt to pass to Eva when you have done with it.
Tell her our G. Mother patched it before she was married.
She was 26 when she married, a wife over 50 years and she
has been in heaven 46 years, so it must be nearly if not quite
100 years old and there is no patchwork like it nowadays...
Your affectionate cousin,

Maggie Headlands (12 November 1908)

Illustration for the cover
of *Girl's Own Annual* by
Kate Greenaway,
London,
late 19th century.
V&A: E.2436-1953

HISTORY OF PATCHWORK

Patchwork is synonymous with the culture of 'make do and mend'. The recycling of scraps of fabric into something which is functional is the embodiment of the thrifty housewife. Victorian artists often used the device of a patchwork quilt to illustrate the most abject scenes of domestic poverty. Equally, the most decorative patchwork is equated with the long leisure hours enjoyed by many middle-class women. For all classes, sewing was an essential part of daily life, both for the making of interior furnishings and the making of clothes. Patchwork was also a commodity. The vogue for making patchwork flourished at the end of the eighteenth century, with the introduction of mass-produced cheap printed cottons. Bags of cotton scraps could be purchased from haberdashers and professional dressmakers, and the most precious fabrics were carefully hoarded – sometimes for years.

The rapidly changing role of middle-class women within the household during the nineteenth century elevated needlework from a pure necessity to a popular and creative diversion. Needlework was also idealized as an important social accomplishment. Small projects such as patchwork could be taken to large social gatherings or smaller, more intimate occasions, and provided an alternative to some of the more interactive occupations such as card playing. Much thought was given to the 'etuis' (also known as 'ladies' companions') – small sewing cases which held a variety of tools and implements, and which were also used to showcase some of the tiny and exquisitely fashioned needle cases and pincushions made by the owner.

Changes in social structures and the availability of cheap, readymade blankets and bed covers lead to a decline in the making of patchwork at the beginning of the twentieth century. The craft revival of the 1970s introduced a new generation to the pleasures of creating innovative patchwork designs – supplied by a seemingly inexhaustible range of specially commissioned fabrics, magazines, books and tools. Yet many continued to use second-hand or recycled fabrics, seeing beauty in the patina of age and wear that old fabrics retain, and in the memories they evoke.

Have you remembered to collect pieces for the patchwork? We are now at a stand-still.

(Jane Austen writing to her sister Cassandra, 1811)

GETTING STARTED

No complicated techniques have been used in this book, and even those with the most rudimentary knowledge of stitching will be able to enjoy making at least one of the five projects. The projects introduce you to the two basic methods of making patchwork:

1. Piecing over papers

This is most commonly known as *mosaic patchwork* but is also referred to as *English paper piecing*. Piecing over paper templates is also invariably associated with the use of hexagons, although it can be used with any tessellating geometric shape, including squares and triangles.

2. Stitching shapes directly together

This technique uses a master template to cut the shapes out of the fabric. It can be used for both hand and machine stitching.

We also introduce you to other methods of using small scraps of fabric such as appliqué, a quick and simple way to decorate your plain patchwork shapes. Like patchwork, appliqué uses templates to create patterns or designs, which are then sewn directly onto a backing cloth or foundation fabric.

All the projects are small enough to work by hand, although instructions on how to piece using a sewing machine are given in Project 3, and instructions for both hand and machine appliqué are provided for Project 4. We suggest you start with the simplest geometric shapes – hexagons, squares and triangles – as these are the easiest to join together. The samples illustrated have all been made by members of the V&A Patchwork Club, all of whom work at the Museum and share their enthusiasm for making patchwork. Template shapes are illustrated for each project, and a sheet with actual size templates is provided at the back of the book.

The opportunities for creating uniquely individual pieces of patchwork are unlimited. The makers of some of the most evocative patchwork pieces in museum collections looked at the world around them, drawing on a wealth of decorative detail to be found in both private and public spheres. We have also provided a selection of images of objects which will give you scope for your creativity – from brightly coloured tiles to beautiful textile designs. A notes section is provided to keep a record of your thoughts, ideas for inspiration and written memories. The aim is to enjoy making patchwork, whether for yourself or as a thoughtful gift for a much-loved friend or relative. The handmade object, although relatively inexpensive in material costs, is always priceless.

'O mother', said Maggie, in a vehemently cross tone, 'I don't want to do my patchwork ... It's foolish work... tearing things to pieces to sew 'em together again'.

(Maggie Tulliver in *Mill on the Floss*, 1880)

CREATING YOUR WORKBOX

Basic patchwork requires little in the way of sophisticated tools and materials. Specialist shops and on-line retailers can supply any number of gadgets and a vast array of fabrics specifically targeted toward the avid patchwork enthusiast. However, for starting off you need little more than a ruler, pencil, scissors and, of course, needle and thread. The more proficient you become, the more likely you are to invest in equipment which will make the more ambitious projects less daunting.

Creating your own personal workbox is part of the fun of making. I was given my first sewing box when I was perhaps 8 or 9 years old. It was filled with reel upon reel of gorgeous coloured cotton and embroidery threads, a little thimble, a packet of 'Sewing Susan' needles and a tiny pincushion. I filled the two drawers with cast-off pearl and glass buttons, miniature packets of sparkling sequins and recycled zips. My grandmother insisted that every last hook and eye should be removed from any cast-off dress or cardigan before it was tossed into the rag bag. I gave my twin daughters their first 'Peter Rabbit workboxes' when they were 6, and today they sit on their desks at university next to the laptop and the MP3 player.

If you are starting from scratch, there are many attractive workboxes on the market. Some will be stocked with the basic tools to start you off on any stitching adventure. The following list is by no means exhaustive but will provide you with everything you need to complete the projects in this book.

Embroidered casket,
English, 1660s.
V&A: T.114-1999

THREAD

Use good-quality cotton thread to match the type of fabric you are using. If you are stitching light-coloured patches to darker ones, use a darker thread as the stitches will be less noticeable. If using more than one colour, you may prefer to use a neutral-coloured thread instead. Do not use invisible thread – you may find it more difficult to handle than cotton thread, and some brands melt when you start to iron your patches.

NEEDLES AND PINS

Blunt needles and pins can mark fabric, so make sure you choose fine, sharp needles and pins to help to make your stitches neat. If you find threading needles too fiddly, invest in a simple needle threader to make life easier.

SCISSORS

A small sharp pair is best for fine work such as cutting threads, while a large, sharp pair is best for cutting out fabric. Do not be tempted to use nail or kitchen scissors. An old pair of scissors should be used for cutting out your paper templates – never use your fabric scissors to cut out paper.

TEMPLATES

These are the patterns for the shapes. There are two ways of using templates:

1. Using a master template to cut out paper templates for each shape when piecing over papers.
2. Using a master template to cut out shapes from fabric when stitching patches together.

You can buy a range of custom-made plastic or metal templates from most haberdashery shops, but the easiest (and cheapest) method is to use thin card. Recycled greetings cards are ideal, and a good way of embracing the thrift revival or 'make do and mend' philosophy. The important thing to remember is accuracy in measuring and cutting out your template and your fabric. Do not be tempted to cut corners – inaccurate patches will not fit together.

THIMBLE

A thimble may seem very old-fashioned, but once you have got used to wearing one it can help to protect your fingers. Make sure it sits securely on the middle finger of your sewing hand.

RULERS

Patchwork requires a high degree of accuracy. A ruler is essential in measuring and ruling your templates and fabrics. Most instructions for patchwork use both metric and imperial measurements, so invest in a ruler that shows both. A word of warning – do not mix up your measurements!

PENCILS

Soft lead pencils are ideal. Remember to keep them sharpened for a fine accurate line.

GRAPH PAPER OR ISOMETRIC (TRIANGULAR GRID) PAPER

We have provided templates for your use at the back of this book. However, if you wish to alter the size of your templates for other projects, copy them onto graph paper and enlarge accordingly. Isometric graph paper is particularly useful for making accurate master templates for hexagons.

OPTIONAL TOOLS

Although not essential, the following items can speed up the preparation of your patches (and help protect your table).

SELF-HEALING CUTTING MAT

Printed with a grid for measuring and cutting fabric, the cheapest versions are available from good stationary stores.

ROTARY CUTTER

If you are embarking on a more ambitious project, such as a bed cover, invest in a good rotary cutter. The sharp cutting blades are invaluable for cutting large quantities of fabric.

Album of dress materials
kept by Barbara Johnson (detail),
British, 1746–1823.
V&A: T.219-1973

FABRIC

Silks for Patchwork – I want pieces of old fashioned brocaded silk and satin to finish quilt begun thirty years ago. I offer in exchange fretwork tools, eccentric monos and badges, tracings from old point and other patterns, modern and classical music. Can send list and other things ... Mag.

(The Queen, The Lady's Newspaper & Court Chronicle, 15 May 1869)

Building up a good collection of fabrics, either new or recycled, will ensure that you will always be able to make something special for birthdays or Christmas, or even to cheer yourself up after a stressful day. Your collection will be an extension of your personality and taste, particularly if you choose to base it on your recycled wardrobe.

Cotton is the easiest fabric to choose for patchwork because it is easy to fold, and washes and wears well. Use the same weight of fabric for your projects, and ensure it is pre-shrunk and colourfast. Mixing natural and synthetic fabric can create quirky effects, but your patchwork may end up puckered and warped because the fabric has different washing instructions. Spend some time making up bundles of co-ordinating scraps for future use – this will help you gain confidence in combining patterns and colourways. Many specialist patchwork suppliers sell pre-cut *fat quarters* (bundles of fabric aimed at the beginner). But be warned – it is very easy to get carried away and end up spending a small fortune on fabulous fabrics.

When choosing patterned fabric for some of the smaller projects, such as the pincushion, we suggest you use small designs, such as florals or checks. Alternating patterned and plain fabrics in matching colour combinations works well together, whilst light and dark tones can help to define a design, particularly in the case of the windmill cot cover (see Project 3).

If using new fabrics, it is a good idea to wash them before embarking on your patchwork. Some fabrics may shrink, or the colours may run. Wash each fabric separately, in warm soapy water followed by a cold rinse. Iron the fabric when dry.

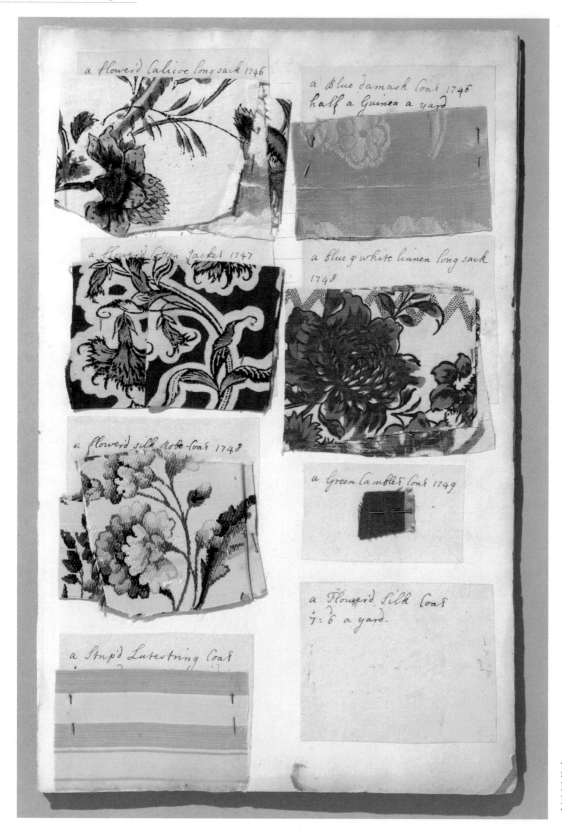

a flower'd Calicoe long sack 1746

a Blue damask Coat 1746
half a Guinea a yard

a flower'd Cotton Jacket 1747

a blue & white linnen long sack
1748

a flower'd silk Robe-Coat 1748.

a Green Cambler Coat 1749

a Flower'd Silk Coat
7: 6 a yard.

a Striped Lutestring Coat

Album of dress
materials kept by
Barbara Johnson,
British, 1746–1823.
V&A: T.219-1973

DEVELOPING YOUR SKILLS

As you become more confident and more proficient at patchwork, you may wish to move on to some of the more technically advanced publications. There are a number of excellent books which will guide you step-by-step through design and an enormous number of patchwork patterns. We have provided a short bibliography at the back of this book, which you may find useful. Alternatively your local library should have one or two beautifully illustrated patchwork books in their craft section.

There are also a number of specialist magazines, which offer advice and provide patterns and templates to copy.

Patchwork classes are a very good way of learning new skills and making new friends – many specialist shops run classes on-site, or can provide you with details of nearby classes.

The Quilters' Guild of the British Isles is an educational charity, which provides educational resources and services for its members. Membership is open to anyone who enjoys making patchwork or appliqué, or quilting, or who has a special interest in quilts. The Guild has a junior branch, the Young Quilters, open to anyone under the age of 16. Contact details for the Quilters' Guild are also provided at the end of this book.

PROJECT 1:

HEXAGON PINCUSHION

HEXAGON PATCHWORK

Patchwork which incorporates the hexagon or honeycomb pattern is inevitably linked with the British tradition of piecing over papers. Although time consuming, hand tacking fabric onto a paper or thin card template guarantees a level of accuracy which is essential in planning the overall design of the patchwork. Many hexagon-based patterns were inspired by mosaic tile designs, popular in nineteenth-century homes and public buildings. In some cases, the piecing over paper technique is referred to as 'English paper piecing', reflecting the diversity and popularity of geometric patterns produced during the period.

Hexagon patchwork is remembered by many as their very first attempt at mastering the art of piecing over paper. Extra curricular activities at school included time to take out your sewing box, to sit and stitch with friends and teachers. Projects included simple keepsakes such as pincushions, lovingly presented to mothers and grandmothers for birthdays and Christmas, or tiny bed covers for dolls' beds. The more skilled and ambitious would move onto patchwork coverlets, recycling fabrics from much-loved dresses which were too small or too worn to hand down to a younger relative.

Although many different patterns can be created using the basic hexagon shape, the most popular is the *rosette*. Relatively easy to design, a central hexagon is surrounded by a circle of six hexagons, cut from variously patterned fabric. Larger rosettes can be created by the addition of a third circle of twelve hexagons. Because the rosettes are relatively small they can be easily carried and stitched on bus and train journeys, in cafes and coffee shops, as well as at home.

The most popular and enduring composition of repeating rosettes is most commonly known as 'Grandmother's Flower Garden'. Many examples made during the nineteenth century contain thousands of hexagons, all neatly overstitched. Each coverlet illustrates the enormous variety of fabrics available, from simple floral repeats to small abstract designs, usually set against a white or neutral ground. In the most exquisite examples, the maker has carefully designed her rosettes so that different floral motifs printed on different fabrics are used for the central hexagon. Other examples combine patterned and plain fabrics, exhibiting an approach to pattern, colour and design which was far ahead of its time.

A popular myth handed down through generations is that women would use their love letters as templates for their patchwork. Many hexagonal coverlets were not lined, indeed some were never finished but were simply put away, to be discovered years later with their papers intact. Close examination reveals that these papers are in fact shopping lists, pages from children's exercise books or templates cut from local broadsheets. Yet the charm of the mythology remains, creating a poignant narrative with each intricately pieced fragment of meaning.

TECHNIQUE: PIECING OVER PAPERS

Working with basic geometric shapes like the hexagon requires accurate cutting out and stitching. The easiest shapes to sew are the ones with wide angles, such as hexagons and octagons. Care must be taken that all the templates are of exactly the same size.

Step 1: Using a master template, make paper templates for each piece of fabric in the design. (See the hexagon template at the back of this book for a basic hexagonal master template.)

Step 2: Lay the fabric right side down and pin a paper template to the centre of the wrong side, with two sides of the hexagon on the straight of grain of the fabric. Include the seam allowance by cutting the fabric around the template ¼ inch (0.6mm) larger than the piece of paper. Fold the seam allowance of one of the straight edges of the fabric over the paper template.

Step 3: Make a knot in the thread and tack through the folded edge of the fabric and paper.

Step 4: Fold the fabric over the next edge and tack through the fold at the corner. Continue like this all round the patch, tacking down each corner.

Step 5: Press the fabric folds. This will make stitching the patches together much easier.

Step 6: Overstitch the patches with right sides together on the wrong side, without catching the papers as you may wish to remove these when the work is finished.

Step 7: Remove the tacking and the paper templates if you wish before lining.

Step 2

Step 3

Step 4

Step 6

Panel of hexagonal
ceramic tiles,
possibly Turkish or
Syrian, 1550–1600.
V&A:908-1894

Printed cotton, 'Brooksby'
by Liberty & Co,
English, c.1910.
V&A: T.311-1976

Printed cotton, 'Daisy'
by Liberty & Co,
English, c.1910.
V&A: T.317-1976

MAKING THE PINCUSHION

She went sometimes to Bristol to buy meal and salt, and she took the opportunity of going to a great many dress-makers, from whom she got a large packet of cuttings, which were too small for general sale.

(Rachel Field, *Polly Patchwork*, 1815)

Fabric pincushions were in household use from at least the sixteenth century. Small decorative versions not only showcased the maker's skill with a needle, but also embodied the good taste and ingenuity required in the conception and execution of beautifully worked and dainty objects. As such, pincushions were popular as courting and wedding presents, christening and New Year's gifts.

Throughout the seventeenth and eighteenth century, pins formed part of the daily routine of dressing, so pin cushions were both practical and decorative. Along with expensive and precious items such as combs, brushes and scent bottles, the cushions would have sat on a lady's dressing table. Originally pins were made by hand, and were expensive items.

Pincushions also represent the intricate rituals that for many centuries surrounded childbirth. At a time when many problems could arise, gifts were presented to celebrate the safe delivery of both mother and child.

This patchwork pincushion provides a simple introduction to piecing over papers, using the basic hexagon shape. This example uses sumptuous cream-coloured velvet as the central hexagon, acquired during a shopping trip to Berwick Street Market in London. The patterned fabrics are off-cuts from a larger dressmaking project. Scrap bags were a feature of every home, including the middle classes, and women were avid collectors of choice snippets of fabrics. Enterprising retailers with an eye to a lucrative market would also supply bags of small remnants to supplement individual hoards. Makers would reserve their most precious fragments, particularly those with emotional resonance, for the central hexagon.

Members of the V&A
Patchwork Club

Step 1: Choose your fabrics and plan your design. Experimenting with colours and patterns can be extremely rewarding, but you may find it easier to focus on just two or three colours that work well together.

Step 2: Use the hexagon template at the back of the book to make a master template. Make fourteen paper templates the same size as the master template.

Step 3: Following the instructions for piecing over papers (p.21), create two rosettes consisting of seven hexagons.

Step 4: Place the rosettes right sides together. Tack all round the rosettes, leaving enough of the hexagon edges free so that the piece can be turned to the right side.

Step 5: Overstitch the rosettes, remembering not to stitch the free edge.

Step 6: Remove papers and turn inside out.

Step 7: Stuff, using wadding.

Step 8: Overstitch the hexagon edge.

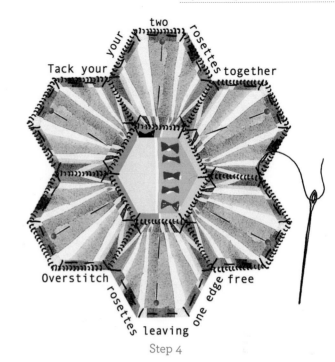

Step 4

PROJECT 2:

SQUARE CUSHION COVER AND PAD

GEOMETRY

Remember that even the smallest scraps left over from your renovations will come in useful for something – patching, tea cosies, coverings for buttons, hanging loops, binding for buttonholes, trimmings, kettle holders, polishers and so on … No doubt there are as many ways of patching or darning as there are of cooking potatoes.

(*Make Do and Mend*, prepared for the Board of Trade by the Ministry of Information, 1943)

The imaginative and inventive use of geometrical patterns is the hallmark of British patchwork. A keen eye can spot the potential for patterns in the most unlikely of places, in the detail of doorways, windows, floor tiles, ironwork and gratings. Ecclesiastical buildings are perhaps the most obvious source for inspiration, from soaring Gothic cathedrals, such as Winchester or Salisbury, to simple parish churches. A single geometric shape can set the basic pattern for cushions or bed covers; combinations of hexagons, squares and triangles can produce endless variations of simple and complicated compositions. The most practical way of achieving an overall decorative effect is to organize the geometric elements into blocks, which can be easily worked on as individual projects. The blocks can then be repeated in rows, checkerboard, in stripes or diagonals.

Playing with shapes and colours is one of the charms of creating patchwork. Choosing a colour palette that reflects your taste and design style makes the patchwork uniquely your own. In the 1970s Laura Ashley's spriggy prints, inspired by nineteenth-century floral fabrics, introduced a new generation to patchwork. Ashley's packages of co-ordinated patchwork squares can still be found in many fabric 'stashes', and are a popular fixture on sites such as ebay, often under the description of 'vintage' fabrics.

Firegrate designed by
Charles Rennie Mackintosh,
Glasgow, 1904.
Circ.244-1963

*Many improvements may be made in the old style of patchwork
that we have been accustomed to see, and, in anticipation of
some improvement in the designs at present used, we venture
to intrude a few remarks, trusting that our 'Family Friends' will
not take them amiss.... The patterns may be varied ad infinitum,
if the person possess the least talent for drawing and designing;
but, for the sake of those who may not be thus gifted, we submit
the accompanying simple and effective design, to be executed in
any of the materials.*

(Godey's Lady's Book, 1850)

Bedroom from
a doll's house,
German, 1920–30.
V&A: B.285-2000

TECHNIQUE: RUNNING STITCH

Patchwork shapes can be sewn directly together using a running stitch. This is an easy way of stitching straight seams, and quicker than piecing over paper. Patchwork can be hand sewn with a running stitch, but can also be machine sewn. The steps below are for hand sewing.

Step 1: Use a master template as a guide to cut out each shape. Allow a ¼ inch (0.6mm) seam allowance around the template shape. You may find it easier to draw a line all around the template with a lead pencil on the wrong side of the fabric, before cutting out the shape, to help you keep your stitches straight and your seam allowance consistent.

Step 2: Pin your patches together, right sides facing, making sure that your pins are at right angles to the straight line.

Step 3: Thread your needle and knot the end.

Step 4: Stitch along the line, using small even stitches.

Step 5: When you have finished, remove the pins
(this is where your pincushion comes in extremely handy).

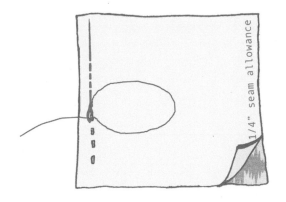

Pachisi game of wood,
straw and cotton,
Indian, 1970s.
V&A: MISC.501-1986

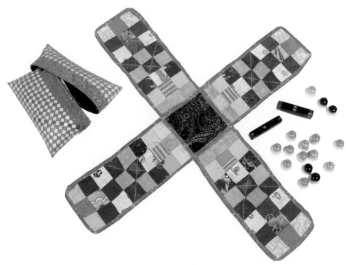

MAKING THE CUSHION COVER AND PAD

The square is perhaps one of the simplest shapes to use in patchwork, and examples often reflect the quirkiness of individual rag bags. A wide variety of printed and plain cottons can be juxtaposed to create an illusion of light and shade. Alternatively, two or three patterns can be combined. Make your own cushion pad using plain cotton and stuffing such as polyester fibrefill. This cushion cover can be hand or machine stitched (see Project 3).

Step 1: Choose your fabrics and plan your design.

Step 2: Use the square shape template at the back of this book to create a master template.

Step 3: Using the master template, cut out nine square patches, remembering to add ¼ inch (0.6mm) seam allowance. If you wish, draw a line around the template with a pencil before cutting out each square. This line is your sewing line.

Step 4: Pin two fabric squares, right sides together. Join using a running stitch, leaving ¼ inch (0.6mm) seam allowance. Pin a third square to one edge. Join and sew as before, making a row of three squares.

Step 5: Press seam allowances to one side (towards the darker fabric).

Step 6: Make three rows of three squares.

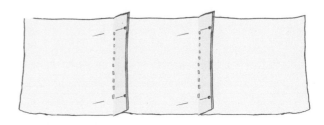

Step 4

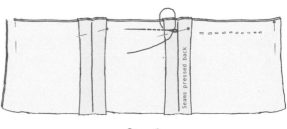

Step 6

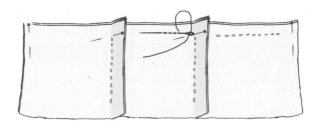

Step 9

Step 7: Pin two rows right sides together, making sure you match up the seams accurately. To reduce bulk where seams cross, press seam allowances in opposite directions, and join using running stitch. Remember to leave your seam allowance and check that your running stitch is straight. Join the third row in the same manner.

Step 8: Press the seams to one side.

Step 9: Using your finished patchwork as a template, cut the backing fabric for your cushion.

Step 10: Pin the backing to the right side of the patchwork and stitch three sides, leaving the fourth open. Turn inside out and press.

Step 11: For the cushion pad, cut two pieces of plain cotton fabric slightly smaller than your patchwork cover. Stitch three sides, leaving the fourth open. Turn inside out.

Step 12: Fill your cushion pad with stuffing, fold in the open edges and stitch over the open edges.

Step 13: Place your cushion pad inside your cover. Fold over the seams of the open edge, and pin together.

Step 14: Overstitch the open edge.

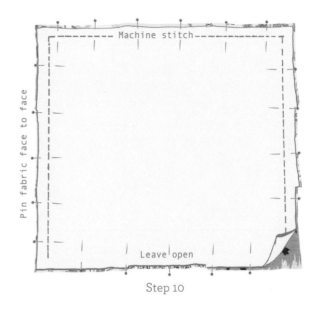

Step 10

Step 14

TIP

Slip some dried lavender between your cushion pad and cover, to make it extra special!

PROJECT 3:

'WINDMILL' COT COVERLET

COT QUILTS AND COVERLETS

Textiles are deeply ingrained in our childhood memories – their touch and smell remind us of our homes, our mothers and the emotional security of our early years. For many, the novelty fabrics of childhood provided an early introduction to the vast array of patterns and colours which populate the world. Brightly coloured figures dancing across cottons are still widely available through department stores, haberdasheries, fabric markets and websites. Cot quilts and coverlets are often kept as treasured heirlooms, as a tactile link to family history. The oral narratives handed down are as precious as the textiles themselves.

The first stages of family life have always been recognized as a cause for celebration. In the seventeenth and eighteenth centuries, aristocratic families marked the birth and survival of a child in a series of rituals which included the presentation of both mother and child. Curtains and bed covers would be brought out of storage, cleaned and hung especially for the occasion. Visitors would be invited in to an intimate chamber to bring gifts and bestow best wishes. Often these evocative textiles would be exchanged between women, a proud declaration of emotional support for a vulnerable new mother and her tiny charge.

Patchwork could also be gifted as tokens of love and friendship. In the eighteenth century sumptuous silk velvets and satins, as well as brightly coloured cottons, were lovingly collected to create small cot quilts for births and christenings. Today patchwork quilts, with their inherent associations of warmth, comfort and security, are still gifted between families and friends on special occasions.

Printed cotton by
the Calico Printers'
Association,
British, 1929.
V&A: T.231-1987

Page from a textile scrap book showing umbrellas, Japanese, 1950s. V&A: FE.23-1997

Printed cotton, 'The House that Jack Built', designed by C.F. Voysey, British, *c.*1929. V&A: T.128-1937.

Illustration, *Baby's Own ABC* by Walter Crane, England, c.1875.
V&A: 123382

TECHNIQUE: MACHINE SEWING

All clothes and household linens were hand sewn until the invention of the sewing machine in the middle of the nineteenth century. By the late 1850s, many of the most affluent homes across Britain were able to purchase a machine. The domestic sewing machine revolutionized the making of patchwork, speeding up the process of stitching. Samuel Beeton, husband of the legendary cookery writer Mrs Beeton and publisher of *The Englishwoman's Domestic Magazine*, started to include paper patterns for both fashion garments and small decorative household items. These pull-outs, familiar to readers of contemporary craft magazines, were a new phenomenon, designed to appeal to the proud owners of the latest domestic tool.

Hand sewing your patchwork can be time consuming, but very therapeutic. Machine sewing can speed up the process, and can be used for larger pieces of fabric and patterns based on squares or triangles.

Step 1: Plan your design before assembling your patches.

Step 2: Pin two patches right sides together – pins should be placed at right angles to the fabric edge. This will make it easier to remove the pins as stitching progresses.

Step 3: Join your patches, using a basic straight stitch on your machine; use the presser foot as a guide to keep your seams straight. You may not need to mark out a straight line with a pencil. On some sewing machines the distance between the needle and the edge of the presser foot of the sewing machine is ¼ inch (0.6mm) which will provide your required seam allowance (please note that machines do vary and you should check this measurement).

Step 4: Continue to join patches together in rows.

Step 5: Press seam allowances to one side (towards the darker fabric).

Step 6: Continue to build up your rows of patches, remembering to take out the pins before they go under the presser foot and to press seams to the side when complete.

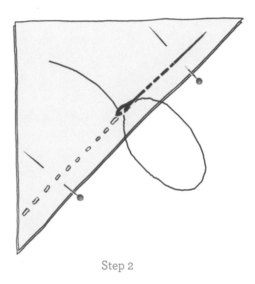

Step 2

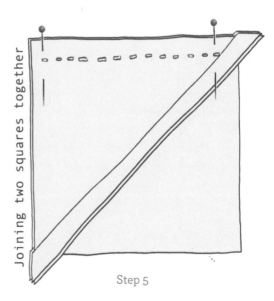

Joining two squares together

Step 5

MAKING THE WINDMILL COT COVERLET

One of the most popular and enduring patchwork designs is the simple repeating triangle commonly known as the 'windmill'. You may choose to work with different patterned fabric, or to alternate two different patterns, to create a spiralling pattern reminiscent of a windmill's gently rotating sails. Alternatively you may decide to work with different shades of one particular colour, for example pink or blue. The wonderful range of novelty fabrics for children will provide you with a wealth of inspiration for creating beautiful heirlooms to welcome the 'sweet babe' into the world.

Step 1: Choose your fabrics – alternating light and dark will add to the charm of the design.

Step 2: Use the triangular template at the back of the book to make a master template.

Step 3: Using the master template, cut eight right-angled triangles, remembering to add ¼ inch (0.6mm) for each seam allowance around each edge. If you wish, draw a line around the master template with a pencil before cutting out each triangle. This line is your sewing line.

Step 4: Hand or machine stitch the triangles together to form one square block. Start by joining two triangles together. Continue to join triangles in pairs until you have four small squares. Join the squares in rows before joining together to form the block.

Step 5: Make an additional three blocks of eight triangles.

Step 6: Join the blocks in two rows of two blocks, then join the two rows together to make one large square.

Step 7: Press your patchwork.

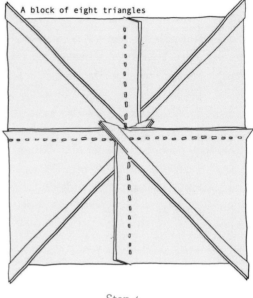

A block of eight triangles

Step 4

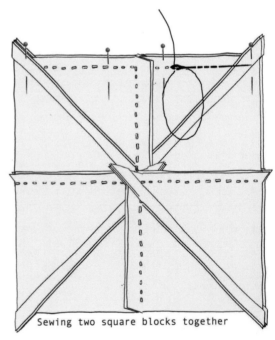

Sewing two square blocks together

Step 6

Step 8: Turn in the raw edges of your patchwork, pin and tack. Press the seam allowance.

Step 9: Prepare your lining. This can be plain or patterned, depending on your taste. Use your patchwork as a template and cut out your lining, remember to include a ¼ inch (0.6mm) seam allowance.

Step 10: Iron your lining, making sure it is smooth.

Step 11: Turn in the raw edges of your lining, pin and tack. Iron the seam allowance.

Step 12: Place the patchwork and lining wrong sides together. Pin and tack all around the edges.

Step 13: Stitch the patchwork and lining together with a single or double row of running stitches (hand or machine stitched).

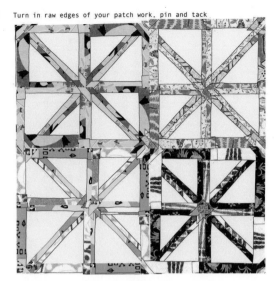

Turn in raw edges of your patch work, pin and tack

Step 8

TIP

For a really special gift, add some beautiful strip binding to your cot cover:

* After attaching the lining, fold the binding over the edges
* Pin, tack and machine stitch in place
* Mitre the corners by folding the binding to make a 90 degree angle

Detail from evening dress designed by the House of Worth, British, c.1955. V&A: T.217-1973

PROJECT 4:
APPLIQUÉ

APPLIQUÉ

Basic appliqué is an easy and fun way to decorate a whole variety of things, such as clothes, shoes, bags, cushions, pillows and bed linen. It can also be used to decorate your patchwork, particularly if you have used plain fabrics. The principle is much the same as patchwork – small pieces of fabric are cut out, using a variety of templates. However, with appliqué the patch is then stitched, or applied, directly onto a background fabric. Appliqué can be more adventurous than patchwork, which relies on the accuracy of its geometric shapes for effect. Templates can be drawn from a wide variety of sources, from children's books, interior magazines, pastry cutters and embroidery designs. The most popular shapes tend to be flowers, leaves, fruit, birds, hearts and animals, but you can draw inspiration from all sorts of everyday objects.

The earliest examples of appliqué were found in the Middle East, Egypt and southern Siberia, on decorated tents, flags and clothing. The technique became very popular in Britain in the seventeenth century, with the introduction of an enormous variety of brightly printed cotton fabrics and *palimpores* (bed covers) from India. The central design of the *palimpore* – a tree of life on a mound, encircled by flowers and exotic birds and set within one or more borders – was extremely influential, and set a trend for appliqué. Many women would cut out the brightly coloured figures and birds from exotic chintz fabrics and apply them to a plain background fabric, creating exquisite bed covers, as well as curtains and wall hangings.

Janet Davis, *Valentine
for Simon Mayes*,
British, 1999.
V&A E.928-2000

TECHNIQUE: APPLIQUÉ

Appliqué can be worked by hand or by machine. You can use cotton fabrics or experiment with a wider range of materials. However, it is better to avoid any fabrics that are likely to fray easily. You will need the same tools as for patchwork, but you can be more adventurous with your templates and take your inspiration from a wide range of sources. You may want to choose a relatively simple shape like a heart or letters of the alphabet, or be more ambitious and create virtual landscapes of figures and animals.

HAND APPLIQUÉ

Step 1: Draw the shape of your design onto paper. If you are using one design several times, you may prefer to draw the template onto card to create a master template.

Step 2: Place the paper template face down, on the wrong side of the fabric. Pin into place. If using a master template, draw around the edge with a sharpened pencil.

Step 3: Cut out the patch, allowing a ¼ inch (0.6mm) seam allowance.

Step 4: Along the curved edges, carefully snip the fabric towards the seam allowance. This will help you turn the fabric under.

Step 5: Fold the seam allowance over the template, and tack in place.

Step 6: Press the edge firmly, then remove tacking stitches and the paper template.

Step 7: Pin each shape in position on your backing fabric, and tack them in place. Oversew them to the background with small stitches, using a thread that matches your appliqué fabric.

Step 8: Remove tacking, and press when sewing is complete.

Step 1

Step 4

Step 5

Step 7

MACHINE APPLIQUÉ

Step 1: Cut out the shape from your template. You do not need a seam allowance.

Step 2: Pin the shape onto your backing fabric.

Step 3: Tack the shape into position.

Step 4: Set your sewing machine to a close zigzag or satin stitch. Place your work under the presser foot with the needle entering at the right hand edge of the fabric to be applied. Your machine will thus be correctly positioned to swing inwards/to the left for the maximum attachment of the piece.

Step 5: Remove tacking stitches, and trim any loose threads or raw edges.

ALTERNATIVE METHOD

An easier way of making appliqué motifs is to use Bondaweb, available from most good haberdashery departments. Bondaweb is an iron-on webbing which can be used to stabilize lightweight fabrics such as rayon and silk.

1. Trace your motifs onto the paper side of the Bondaweb, and then cut around the shapes. Place the motifs onto the wrong side of your chosen fabric, with the adhesive facing downwards. Press on your motif.

2. Cut out your motif as accurately as you can, and peel off the backing paper. Lay your motifs right side up onto your backing fabric.

3. When you are happy with your design layout, carefully press again. You can now stitch around your motifs, using a matching or contrasting thread. For best results, read the instructions on the Bondaweb packet.

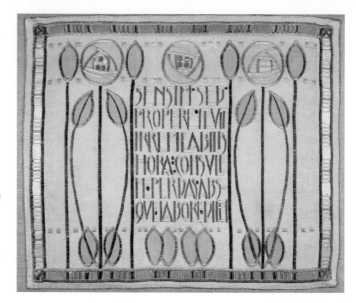

Embroidered cushion cover, British, c.1900. V&A: T.69-1953

Appliqué coverlet of
printed cottons,
British, c.1851.
V&A: T.86-1957

UNUSUAL PATTERNS AND MATERIALS

CRAZY

Crazy patchwork became extremely popular in the nineteenth century, when more elaborate fabrics such as velvet, brocade and silk – as well as a wide range of braids and ribbons – became more widely available. It took its name from the seemingly random placement of irregular shaped fabrics embellished with decorative embroidery stitches, such as herringbone and feather stitch.

The introduction of aniline dyes created a wealth of vivid and eye-catching colours, which heralded a return to luxury and excess within the home. The jewel-like sheen of the dyes on silk and the brightly coloured embroidery threads, juxtaposed with the haphazard placement of scraps and fragments, created a feast for the eye which was truly 'crazy'.

Crazy patchwork was used for large and small household items, including quilts, cushions, piano covers, table covers, and more intimate possessions such as theatre or work bags. Magazines such as *Weldon's Practical Guide to Needlework* and *The Englishwoman's Domestic Magazine* illustrated examples of what was sometimes described as 'kaleidoscope' patchwork. The more eccentric pieces also included additional embroidery and decoration in the form of beading and sequins, and sometimes 'found' objects such as feathers and shells. Although 'crazy' patchwork was considered by some to be the height of fashion, some had serious reservations about the quality of the work. In her book *Decorative Art of Victoria's Era* (1950), Frances Lichten condemned crazy patchwork as 'the supreme efflorescence of tastelessness'!

Detail of man's wool jacket,
Algerian, late 19th century.
V&A: T.117-1916

TECHNIQUE: CRAZY PATCHWORK

The joy of crazy patchwork is that you do not have to be bound by any rules. Your fabric shapes do not need to be accurate, your stitches do not need to be the same size, and mistakes are easily covered up with surface decoration such as additional embroidery or appliqué. The aim is to be as inventive and creative as you can!

Step 1: Crazy patchwork pieces are sewn onto a foundation fabric, so lightweight fabrics are ideal for this. Place your first scrap of fabric right side up onto your chosen backing fabric.

Step 2: Tack in place.

Step 3: Place your second scrap of fabric right side up along one edge of the first scrap. Turn in the raw edge with the second scrap, place over the raw edge of the first scrap, and tack in place.

Step 4: Continue to cover the backing fabric with scraps.

Step 5: Embroider each seam using herringbone, feather, button hole or chain stitch, using different coloured embroidery thread.

Step 6: Remove tacking stitches.

Turn in raw edge of second scrap on the edge where it meets the first scrap.

Step 3

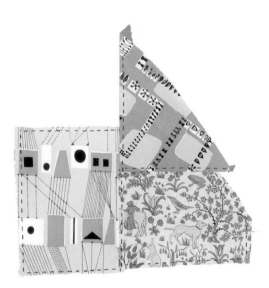

Step 4

Left: Pedlar doll
made of white kid,
English, 1830.
V&A: MISC.1-1924

Right: Detail from
Lady Clapham doll,
English, 1690–1700.
V&A: T.846-1974

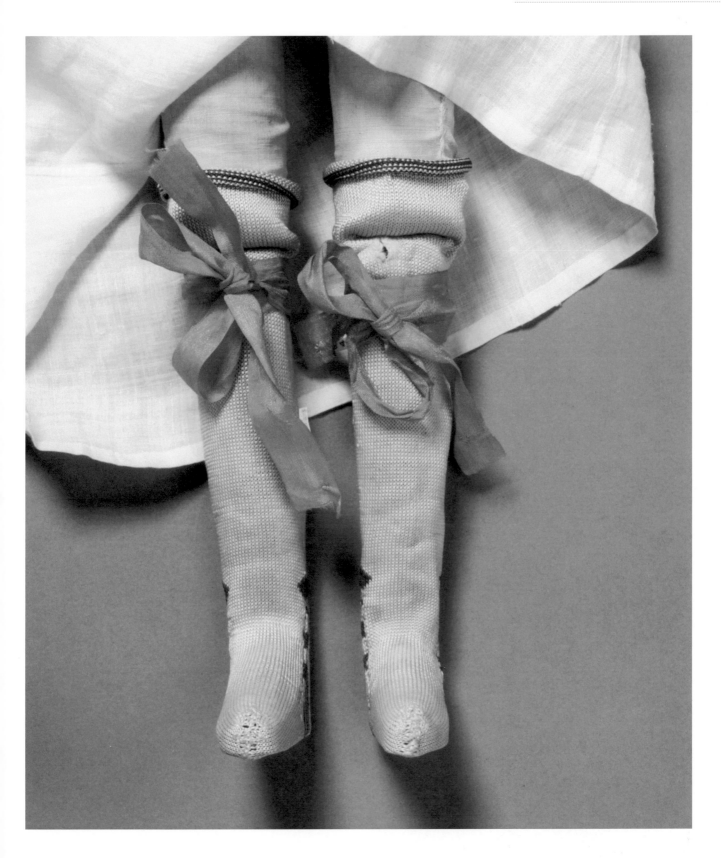

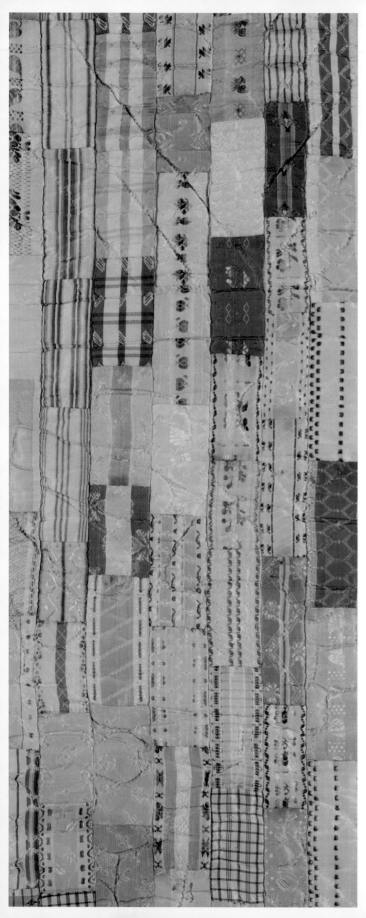

STRIP PATCHWORK

As an alternative, strip patchwork is an excellent way of using strong vertical strips of bold or contrasting fabrics. It is also ideal for recycling materials from old clothes, such as strips of fabric cut from altered dresses or even zips removed from jackets and trousers. Silk ribbons, cotton dresses, flannel bedding, tweed jackets or suiting have all been lovingly pieced into patchwork over the years.

RIBBONS STRIP PATCHWORK

It was a fine silken thing which I espied walking the other day through Westminster Hall, that had as much ribbon about him as would have plundered six shops and set up Twenty Country Peddlars. All his body was dres't like a Maypole.

(John Evelyn, 1661)

The increased availability of ribbons from the late seventeenth century led to widespread adornment. Both men and women engaged in the craze for unabashed decoration. Lovers of the most delicious and desirable decorative ribbons would incorporate them into their patchwork projects, creating whole quilts out of intricate and delicate confections, strewn with glinting silver threads.

Start collecting scraps of gorgeous silks and luscious brocades, and save all the lovely ribbons which are used to wrap your luxury chocolates and sensuous bath products. Your strip patchwork can be your fabric diary, documenting all your birthdays and Christmas presents – with some added sparkle!

You can use the same basic 'crazy' technique of sewing onto a foundation cloth to create your ribbon strip patchwork.

Quilted patchwork bedcover
made of silk and brocaded ribbons
English, 1740-1800
V&A: T.117-1973

Step 1: Choose your background fabric.

Step 2: Collect your ribbons and fabric strips.

Step 3: Place your first ribbon on your background fabric, right side up.

Step 4: Place your second ribbon wrong side down over the first ribbon, lining up one edge.

Step 5: Sew along this one edge, through both ribbons and the background fabric.

Step 6: Flip the second ribbon over to its right side. Press it in place with your finger so it lies flat.

Step 7: Place your third ribbon wrong side down over the second ribbon, and sew, flip and press in the same way.

Step 8: Continue in this way until you have the covered the width of your fabric.

Step 9: Start your second row of ribbons and continue until you have covered the whole of your background fabric.

ALTERNATIVE METHOD

You can also use the 'stitch and flip' method for crazy patchwork:

1. Choose your first crazy scrap and trim it so that it has an odd number of edges.

2. Choose your second scrap and trim it, so that it has one side the same length as the longest side of the first scrap.

3. Place right sides together and stitch through scraps and background fabric. Continue to add scraps, working in a clockwise manner.

Detail from silk satin doublet,
English, 1630s.
V&A: 347-1905

Silk busk and stays,
English, 1660–70.
V&A: T.14-1951

TEMPLATES

FURTHER INFORMATION

FURTHER READING

There are many excellent books available from bookshops and on-line. Here are a few to get you started.

Adele Corcoran & Caroline Wilkinson.
Mini Quilts from Traditional Designs.
Sterling Publishing (1995)

Lynne Edwards.
The Sampler Quilt Book.
David & Charles PLC (2002)

Katharine Guerrier.
Scrap Quilt Projects: Easy Mini Gifts to Make and Sell.
Rainbow Discs (2008)

Elaine Hammond.
The Absolute Beginner's Guide to Patchwork.
David & Charles PLC (1997)

Linda Seward.
The Complete Book of Patchwork, Quilting and Appliqué.
Mitchell Beazley (2009)

SPECIALIST SHOPS

You can find specialist shops throughout the country. Here are a few suggestions:

LONDON

Fabrics Galore:
54 Lavender Hill,
London SW11 5RH

SOUTH

Quilt Room:
20 West Street,
Dorking RH4 1BL

EAST

Sew and So's:
14 Upper Olland Street,
Bungay, Suffolk NR35 1BG

WEST

Country Threads:
2 Pierrepont Place,
Bath, BA1 1JX

MIDLANDS

The Cotton Patch:
1283-1285 Stratford Road, Hall Green,
Birmingham B28 9AJ

NORTH

Fat Quarters:
5 Chopwell Road, Blackhall Mill,
Newcastle on Tyne NE17 7TN

SCOTLAND

Mandors:
131 East Claremont St, Edinburgh, EH7 4JA

ORGANISATIONS

The following organisations can put you in touch with patchwork and quilting groups in your area

The Quilters' Guild of the British Isles,
St Anthony's Hall, York, YO1 7PW
www.quiltersguild.org.uk

City and Guilds Level 3 Certificate in
Design and Craft: Patchwork and Quilting
City & Guilds Head Office, 1 Giltspur Street,
London EC1A 9DD
www.cityandguilds.com

ACKNOWLEDGEMENTS

I would like to thank Linda Seward, Dorothy Osler and Diana Springall for their technical input to this publication. Thanks also to Linda Parry and Caroline Wilkinson for their help and advice. Enormous thanks to the V&A Patchwork Club for their enthusiasm and support for this project, with particular thanks to Michelle Jensen for her keen eye and for supplying the beautiful workboxes for the photo shoot. Thanks also to Sarah Sevier for collaborating with the styling for each project. The author acknowledges the help and support of Turnbull Grey, Miranda Harrison, Polly Scott Bolton, Peter Kelleher, Richard Davis, Pip Barnard and Anjali Bulley. Finally, this book would not have happened without the dedication, good humour and unwavering support of Claire Smith.

For Pippi, who taught me how to stitch

Sue Prichard

NOTES